PICASSO

PICASSO MUSEUM, BARCELONA

Photographic report, complemented
by a biography of the painter

Text by XAVIER COSTA CLAVELL

Photographs, lay-out and reproduction, entirely design-
ed and created by the Technical Department of EDITO-
RIAL ESCUDO DE ORO, S.A.

Editorial Escudo de Oro, S.A.

Corrida and six studies of doves, works created by Picasso in Málaga in 1890. (20.2 × 13.1 cm). Picasso Museum, Barcelona.

THE GENIUS OF PICASSO

One kind of painting was practised before the appearance of Picasso. After the revolutionary intervention in the world of plastic arts of the genius from Málaga, there was another type of painting. As the author of *Guernica* himself said, ''We now know that art is not truth. Art is a lie that makes us realise truth, at least the truth which is given us to understand (...) The artist must find the way of convincing the public of the entire veracity of his lies.'' The great painter was always substantially faithful to the creative co-ordinates underlying this idea; Picasso's artistic adventures followed this orientation throughout his different periods and experiences.

To find figures comparable with Picasso in the history of universal painting, one must refer to Leonardo da Vinci, Giotto, Velázquez and Goya — to the great artists who made innovations in creative conceptions in their respective periods and opened up new paths in the field of plastic arts. Picasso never followed the beaten track, nor was he content with the innumerable admirable discoveries with which his oeuvre is marked: ''I do not search, I find,'' he said. He always advanced, despite what might seem to be indicated to the contrary by his enriching variations

Portrait of the artist's friend Pallarès, painting. *Pencil drawing, Barcelona, 1895. (30.8 × 23.8 cm). P.M.B.*

Copy of a plaster cast. Art school drawing in *charcoal, Barcelona, 1895. (62.5 × 47.5 cm). P.M.B.*

Agile sketch of the artist's father. *Pencil drawing, Barcelona, 1895. (19.5 × 13.5 cm). P.M.B.*

on one theme. When Picasso was 76 — and had for many years justly been considered the greatest painter of the 20th century — he stated that, "Everything I have done is just the first step on a long path. It is only a preliminary process, which must be developed much later on. My works must therefore be considered each in relation to the others, always taking into account what I have done and what I am going to do."

Picasso's life — the environments he lived in, his love affairs, his ideas, his profoundly Spanish roots, his settling in France — is intimately linked with his artistic work, influencing it in one way or another and always enriching it. He was a profoundly humane artist, in whom intuition was always overwhelmingly predominant over theoretical knowledge. His biography is thus absolutely crucial if one wishes to penetrate the complex content of his oeuvre. It was not in vain that the painter himself declared: "I do not develop, I am."

The artist was born in Málaga on October 25th 1881. The birth was at 9.30 p.m. (according to Picasso himself, although Palau i Fabre wrote in *The Extraordinary Life of Picasso* that it was at 11.15), in number 36 (now 16), Plaza de la Merced in the beautiful provincial capital. As Palau i Fabre wrote in

Family scene. *Oil on canvas, painted in Corunna or Barcelona in 1895. (13.8 × 22.1 cm). P.M.B.*

the aforementioned work, "It was a bad delivery and the midwife took no notice of him, thinking he was dead, but his uncle Salvador, a doctor, blew smoke in his face from the cigarette he was smoking and made him cry. That is how Picasso managed to stay alive." The new-born child was baptised with the name Pablo.

The parents of the great painter-to-be were called José Ruiz Blasco and María Picasso López. His father, an art teacher, was forty when the author of *Les Demoiselles d'Avignon* was born. He was a tall, blond man with a happy, good-natured personality; his family was apparently from New Castile and Aragon. The mother, on the other hand, was a brunette; her beautiful dark eyes shone with a lively expression. According to Pierre Daix, "Her family had settled in Málaga long before, although their Andalusian origins cannot be established with certainty. The spelling of the surname is strange in Spanish, due to the double s; although an Italian painter called Matteo Picasso, who lived in Genoa last century, has been discovered, there is however no reason allowing us to suspect possible Italian ancestry." The couple also had two daughters, Lola, born in 1884, and Concepción ('Concha'), in 1887.

Jaime Sabartés (whose life was closely linked with Picasso's) and some of the painter's Catalan friends insisted on more than one occasion that Picasso was much more like his mother than his father. Referring to the artist's mother, Sabartés said that "Doña María's virtues made her more beautiful — she was good-natured, intelligent, a model of gracefulness and wit; but Don José's character, sharpness and personality matched his wife's merits and qualities... It was undoubtably from his mother, nevertheless, that Picasso inherited the refinement, good temper and natural grace that characterise him. If, however,

Copy of a fragment of Estudi de Mas Fontdevila. *Oil on panel, Barcelona, 1895. (22.3 × 13.7 cm). P.M.B.*

La virgen me perdone *("May the Virgin Mary forgive me")*. Pencil and watercolour, Barcelona, 1895-96. (27.5 × 19.7 cm). P.M.B.

Sketch for Vieja recibiendo aceite de un monaguillo *("Old Woman receiving Oil from an Altar Boy")*. Pen and ink, Barcelona, 1895-96. (20.8 × 15.9 cm). P.M.B.

Vieja recibiendo aceite de un monaguillo *("Old Woman receiving Oil from an Altar Boy")*. Oil on canvas affixed to board, Barcelona, 1896. (29.2 × 20.2 cm). P.M.B.

we observe his involuntary expressions when he is nervous, impatient, tired or annoyed, when people importune him, when something interrupts his work, we can recognise Don José; but with one difference — what irritated his father was actually painting!"

Pablo Picasso, on the contrary, felt an overriding necessity to paint, throughout his life. Painting was his reason for living, and also his greatest joy: thence the playful spirit reflected in his best works.

The family moved to La Coruña (Corunna) in September 1891. It seems that they were not at all enthusiastic about the move. But, as Pablo Picasso was to recall many years later, "Although my father felt

very disheartened, for me the journey to Corunna was great fun." They travelled from Málaga to Vigo by boat, and continued by land to the capital of the province. Picasso was almost ten years old; he felt happy contemplating the green landscapes of Galicia.

The Ruiz Picasso family occupied number 14, Calle Payo Gómez Charino, a three-storey stone building where in 1971 a marble tablet was placed, reading: "Pablo Ruiz Picasso lived and painted in this house, 1891-1895."

These four years in the painter's life have not been extensively studied; the period spent in the Galician capital is, however, of considerable importance in his

Detail of Houses. *Oil on canvas, Barcelona, 1896. (23.5 × 29.4 cm). P.M.B.*

Beach. *Oil on canvas, Barcelona, 1896. (24.4 × 34 cm). P.M.B.*

Salón del Prado. *Oil on panel, Madrid, 1896 or 1897. (10 × 15.5 cm). P.M.B.*

development, for it was in Corunna that Picasso began to demonstrate his extraordinary faculties. His father had taught him to draw; one day, when the family was living in Corunna, as Palau i Fabre wrote, ''There occurred an unwonted event: the father, the teacher, realised that his son, the pupil, knew more than him, and that he could not teach him any more

Hombre apoyado en un portal gótico (*"Man leaning in a Gothic Doorway"). Oil on canvas, Barcelona, 1896. (20.2 × 12.8 cm). P.M.B.*

Corner of San Pablo del Campo cloister. *Oil on panel, Barcelona, 1896. (15.5 × 10.1 cm). P.M.B.*

— not only that, but that his son could give him lessons. That day Don José handed over his brushes, his palette, his easel, all his painting instruments, to his son, and never painted again. From then on he only used his pencils for correcting his pupils' drawings in class.''

It was also in Corunna that Picasso had his first exhibition. Later, when he was famous, he asked on several occasions whether there were drawings by him in the Galician city, saying that there must be many.

The Orzán bay and Hercules' Tower, Picasso was to say, ''are dearly beloved places for me.'' At thirteen years of age he wrote, as the caption of a caricature in which he had drawn skirts swirling in the storm *(O vento do Fisterre zoando alporizado)*, ''The wind has

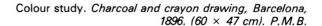

Colour study. *Crayon drawing, Barcelona, 1896. (47.5 × 31 cm). P.M.B.*

Colour study. *Charcoal and crayon drawing, Barcelona, 1896. (60 × 47 cm). P.M.B.*

Sketch of the Painter's Mother, his Sister Lola, and two Hands. *Pen and ink, Barcelona, 1895-96. (22.1 × 16.2 cm). P.M.B.*

got up in turn, and will continue blowing until there is no trace of Corunna.''

Although he had already begun in Málaga, it was in the Galician period (1891-1895) that Picasso really devoted himself to drawing doves, his symbol that with time was to become the representation of universal love of peace. Another interesting facet of the painter's restless activity in the four years he lived in Corunna was the creation of magazines of only one copy, which he edited, directed, wrote and illustrated, such as ''Torre de Hércules,'' ''La Coruña'' and ''Azul y Blanco.''

Corunna thus has the honour of being the city that as it were fostered the artist as a child, the environment where Pablo Picasso's creative genius began to crystallise.

Picasso's youngest sister, Concepción, died in Corunna towards the end of 1894; in October the following year his father took up his appointment at the School of Fine Arts in Barcelona, exchanging his post in the Galician capital with a teacher named Novarro García. The move to Barcelona was to prove decisive in Picasso's artistic training. In 1895 he was admitted to La Lonja, where his father taught: he passed the entrance examination without any difficulty.

Pablo Picasso's first studio was in Calle de la Plata; he shared it with Manuel Pallarès. The artist worked extremely hard in this period; in the words of Palau i Fabre, ''These were months of intensive, compelling, almost violent work, as was to be the case throughout his life.'' In 1897 he painted *Science and Charity*: this work obtained honourable mention at the General Exhibition of Fine Arts in Madrid. In the same year Picasso entered the Academia de Bellas Artes de San Fernando. Soon afterwards, however, he fell ill; by invitation of his friend Pallarès, he rested for some time at the latter's house in Horta d'Ebre, a village in the district of Terra Alta. Later, Picasso was

The Artist's Father. *Pen, ink and aquatint, Barcelona, 1895-96. (15 × 16.5 cm). P.M.B.*

Portrait of María Picasso López, the Artist's Mother, in Profile. *Watercolour, pen and ink, and pencil, Barcelona, 1896. (18 × 12.5 cm). P.M.B.*

Portrait of María Picasso López, the Artist's Mother. *Pastel, Barcelona, 1896. (49.8 × 39 cm). P.M.B.*

to comment that "All that I know, I learned in Horta d'Ebre." He painted *Aragonese Customs* there: it won a medal in Madrid and another in the city where the artist was born, Málaga.

When Picasso had recovered from his illness he returned to Barcelona, where he made contact with the lively group of artists who used to meet in Els Quatre Gats ("The Four Cats"), a popular establishment run by Pere Romeu. His friendship with Jaime Sabartés, the sculptor Manolo, the painter Junyer, Casagemas, Reventós and others dated from this period.

Picasso's first exhibition in Barcelona, precisely at "Els Quatre Gats," was in February 1900. With reference to this exhibition, as Palau i Fabre wrote, "Rodríguez Codolá published an extensive, highly favourable article in 'La Vanguardia' on February 3rd 1900, commenting on the painting of this eighteen-year-old youth — he was the first to perceive his genius."

This was a particularly felicitous period in Picasso's life. He left us valuable testimony of these happy days: a pen drawing showing the artist, surrounded by a group of friends seated drinking and smoking

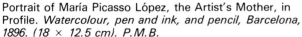 The First Communion. *Oil on canvas, Barcelona, 1896. (166 × 118 cm). P.M.B.*

Portrait of José Ruiz Blasco, the Artist's Father.
Watercolour, Barcelona, 1896. (18 × 11.8 cm). P.M.B.

The Artist's Father. *Watercolour, Barcelona, 1896.*
(25.5 × 17.8 cm). P.M.B.

around a table, with his black hair dishevelled, bearded, with overcoat and stick, and wearing a large hat.

Picasso was nineteen when, accompanied by his friend Casagemas (who committed suicide in 1901), he undertook the adventure of conquering Paris, at that time the artistic capital of Europe. The two friends set up their studio at number 49 rue Gabrielle, ceded to them by Isidro Nonell, who had decided to return to Barcelona. Two months later Picasso signed a contract with the Catalan art dealer Pere Manyac, undertaking to deliver all the work he produced in return for 150 francs a month.

In the fascinating atmosphere of Paris at the beginning of the century, Picasso soon became one of the most active residents of Montmartre. He lived in the famous Bateau-Lavoir until 1904, alongside such figures as André Salmon, Cornelius van Dongen and

Juan Gris; but resided alternately in Paris and Barcelona. This was the beginning of Picasso's Blue Period, which was to last from the end of 1901 to early 1905.

Picasso visited Málaga at the end of 1901. A few days later he was in Madrid, where with Francisco Soler he founded the short-lived magazine *Arte Joven* ("Young Art"). In April of the same year he moved to Barcelona and exhibited a series of pastels in the Sala Parés: they were glowingly appraised by Miguel

Utrillo in *Pel i Ploma*. The painter returned to Paris in May and held a joint exhibition of 75 works with Iturrino in the gallery of the famous art dealer Ambroise Vollard.

In 1904, when living at the Bateau-Lavoir, Picasso met the poet Apollinaire. In this period he began to be very interested in the world of the circus: he incorporated circus figures into his paintings, thus beginning the Rose Period. This was also the time he began to sell his works to North American buyers (Gertrude

Self-Portrait. *Oil on panel, Barcelona, 1896. (22.1 × 13.7 cm). P.M.B.*

Self-Portrait with Wig. *Oil on panel, Barcelona, 1896. (55.8 × 46 cm). P.M.B.*

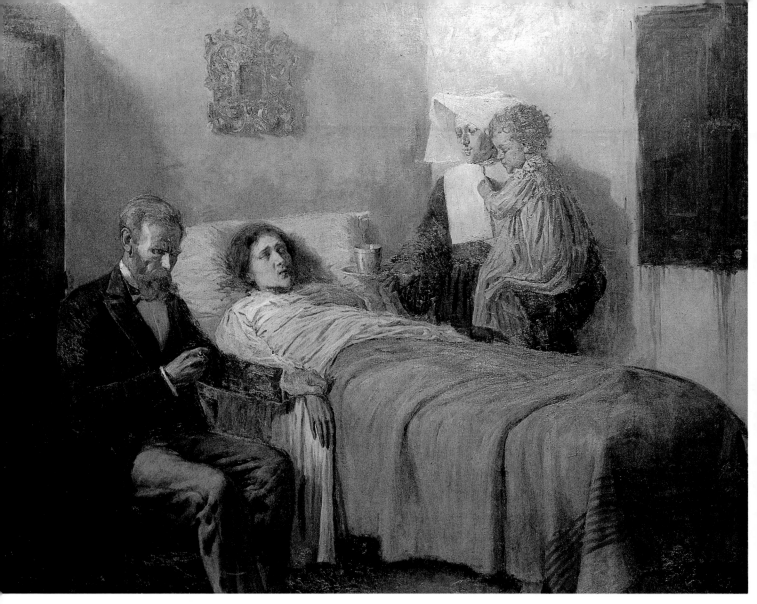

Science and Charity. *Oil on canvas, Barcelona, 1897.*
(197 × 249.5 cm). P.M.B.

Stein, among others), and when he met Fernande Olivier, with whom he was to establish one of his longest, and artistically most fruitful, love affairs. At that time Fernande was experiencing the drama of seeing her sculptor husband succumbing to madness, and her relationship with Picasso did not commence until later on, towards the end of the Rose Period. She left us an invaluable written description of Picasso at the beginning of the century: in her eyes he was "Small, dark, thick-set, restless, disquieting, with eyes dark, profound, piercing, strange, almost staring. Awkward gestures, the hands of a woman, poorly dressed, badly groomed. A thick lock of hair, black and shining, slashed across his intelligent and obstinate forehead. Half bohemian, half workman in his dress, his long hair brushed the collar of his worn-out jacket...."

Picasso's personal and artistic character was becom-

Sketch for Science and Charity. *Oil on panel, Barcelona,* 1897. (19.5 × 27.2 cm). P.M.B.

Sketch for Science and Charity. *Oil on canvas, Barcelona,* 1897. (23.8 × 26 cm). P.M.B.

Sketch for Science and Charity. *Oil on panel, Barcelona,* 1897. (13.6 × 22.4 cm). P.M.B.

Sketch for Science and Charity. *Watercolour, Barcelona,* 1897. (22.8 × 28.4 cm). P.M.B.

ing firmly defined in this period. As well as frequenting foreign figures of the world of art and literature who came to the Bateau-Lavoir (Max Jacob, Apollinaire, Van Dongen and many other names that are famous nowadays), the painter from Málaga surrounded himself with Spaniards resident in Paris. They formed the group known as "La Bande Picasso": the sculptors Manolo Hugué and Paco Durrio, the painters Ignacio Zuloaga, Ricardo Canals, Ramon Pitxot, and others.

1907 was a particularly interesting, significant year in Picasso's artistic development. That spring he painted one of his most famous canvases, *Les Demoiselles d'Avignon*. This work has no direct rela-

Street Violinist. *Pencil and watercolour, Madrid, 1897-98. (23.5 × 33.5 cm). P.M.B.*

Couple from Behind. *Pencil, Madrid, 1897-98. (24.3 × 16.5 cm). P.M.B.*

Brawl in a Café. *Black and red crayon, Barcelona, 1897-99. (22.9 × 33.5 cm). P.M.B.*

La Chata. *Charcoal, watercolour and gouache, Barcelona, 1899. (31.6 × 7.6 cm). P.M.B.*

tion with the city of Avignon in France, but was a result of the artist's memories of a certain brothel located in Carrer Aviñó, Barcelona. This is often cited as the starting point of Picasso's Cubist phase. In the same year the painter entered into relations with Georges Braque and Kahnweiler, who was to become his exclusive dealer.

It was also in this period that Picasso began to be interested in Negro art: its naive, profound expressiveness was to open up new seams of inspiration for him. Cubism and Negro art were the predominant influences in these years of intense work for the painter. His aesthetic conception was constantly enriched and renewed; his technique reached a point of unsurpassable perfection. In this period Picasso's creations were clearly shaped by his theoretical preoccupations. His fascinating Analytical Cubism was to be prolonged until 1911, when it gave way to rigorous conceptualism, admirably expressed in his work.

These were extraordinarily busy years in Picasso's life; he visited Barcelona on several occasions. The artist spent the summer of 1909 at Horta d'Ebre, in the company of Fernande Olivier. That same year he exhibited works at the Tannhäuser Gallery in Munich. In 1910 he stayed at Cadaqués for a while, accompanied by Fernande Olivier and Derain, and painted several Cubist portraits, among them that of Vollard. Picasso spent the three following summers at Céret, with Manolo Hugué, Braque, Juan Gris and Max Jacob. His father died in 1913. A year earlier a new woman had appeared in Picasso's life: Marcelle Humbert. He called his lover Eva; she died in hospital towards the end of 1915. Curiously enough, Picasso never painted Marcelle, although he made many portraits of his other companions. In 1912 he had exhibit-

The Divan. *Charcoal, pastel and crayon, Barcelona, 1899.*
(25 × 29 cm). P.M.B.

The Artist's
Sister Lola.
*Charcoal and
crayon,
Barcelona,
1899.
(44 × 29 cm).
P.M.B.*

Two sketches of Seated Women. Pencil on cover of a notebook, Barcelona, 1899. (23 × 16.8 cm). P.M.B.

Seated Woman, reading. *Watercolour, Barcelona, 1899. (19 × 14 cm). P.M.B.*

ions at the Stafford Gallery in London and at Galerías Dalmau in Barcelona.

Picasso's friends were dispersed when the tragedy of the First World War broke out. The only ones to remain in Paris were the sculptor Gargallo and Max Jacob, who was certified unfit for military service.

In 1916, at the height of the war, Jean Cocteau put Picasso into contact with Diaghilev and the leading members of the Ballets Russes. The artist collaborated with them by designing the sets, costumes and curtain for *Parade* and the sets of *Three-Cornered Hat* and *Pulcinella.* Picasso's work with the magnificent Russian dance group, which was to extend over several years, enabled him to make friends with the great ballerina Olga Koklova: they were married in 1918, with Max Jacob and Jean Cocteau as best men.

At the end of the war, Picasso was attracted to the Surrealist movement: he carried out audacious explorations in the plastic arts. André Breton himself

Portrait of Sebastián Junyer Vidal, in profile. *Lead pencil, crayons and watercolour on glazed paper, Barcelona, 1899. (21 × 16 cm). P.M.B.*

Portrait of Carlos Casagemas. *Oil on canvas, Barcelona, 1899. (55 × 45 cm). P.M.B.*

later declared in his essay *Le Surréalisme et la Peinture,* "That the position held by us now could have been delayed or lost depended only on a failure in the determination of this man. His admirable perseverance was for us such a valuable pledge that we do not need to recur to any other authority."

1924 was another important year in Picasso's artistic development: he began the series of still lifes that continued in 1925. The artist took part in the exhibition of Surrealist paintings organised at Galerie Pierre Loeb in Paris in 1925.

In 1931 he illustrated Balzac's *Le Chef-d'oeuvre Inconnu* ("The Unknown Masterpiece") and Ovid's *Metamorphoses;* from 1927 to 1937 he created the extraordinary series of etchings — about a hundred — known as the *Vollard Suite.*

In 1935 Picasso and Olga Koklova separated: he applied for a divorce, but his wife refused. That same year Maïa, his daughter by Marie-Thérèse Walter, was born. Picasso had met Marie-Thérèse by chance; the full curves of her body were the inspiration for several superb sculptures. Still in 1935, the poet Paul Eluard introduced him to Dora Maar, a painter and photographer active in Surrealist circles: Picasso's relationship with her lasted for some years, and he painted several magnificent portraits of her. It was also in 1935 that he engraved the *Minotauromachie* series, and that his friend Jaime Sabartés became his secretary.

Picasso was appointed Director of the Prado Museum in 1936. The following year he painted *Guernica,* his most famous picture, commissioned by the

Republican Government of Spain, in which he symbolised the horrors of war, based on the brutal destruction of this Basque city by the Nazi air force. Picasso presented a magnificent exhibition at the Museum of Modern Art in New York in 1939. His satisfaction with the resounding success of the exhibition was diminished by his mother's death towards the end of the Spanish Civil War.

Picasso was at Royan in France in 1940 when Hitler's troops occupied the town. His secretary Sabartés recorded the painter's comments: ''They are another race... They think they are very smart and maybe they are; they have made progress... It is true, but so what? In any case, we certainly paint better than they do. At bottom, if you look carefully, they are very stupid. All those troops, those machines, that power and that uproar to get here! We arrived with less noise... What nonsense! Who was preventing them from acting like us? Maybe they think they have conquered Paris. But we took Berlin a long time ago, without moving from here, and I don't think they will be able to eject us from there.'' Picasso was trying to be optimistic, but at bottom he was deeply upset by the German troops' occupation.

In 1946 Picasso met Françoise Gilot, who was to be his companion for some years. After their liaison was

Nude Woman from behind. *Pencil, Barcelona, 1899. (61.8 × 47.5 cm). P.M.B.*

Carter. *Pencil, Barcelona, 1897-99. (32.1 × 24.6 cm). P.M.B.*

Nude Woman, seated. *Pencil, Barcelona, 1899. (47.6 × 31.6 cm). P.M.B.*

Picador and monosabio (assistant). *Pen, ink and watercolour, Barcelona, 1899. (33.8 × 23.4 cm). P.M.B.*

over, Gilot published a fierce book about her relations with Picasso (as did Fernande Olivier), in which she described the artist as follows: "Dark hair, bright flashing eyes, very squarely built, rugged — a handsome animal. Now, his greying hair and absent look — either distracted or bored — gave him a withdrawn, Oriental appearance that reminded me of the statue of the Egyptian scribe in the Louvre. There was nothing sculptural or fixed in his manner of moving, however: he gesticulated, he twisted and turned, he got up, he moved rapidly back and forth."

Picasso participated in the Salon d'Automne for the first time in 1944, presenting over 70 works. In 1947 he became keenly interested in pottery. He settled at Vallauris (a town that was to name him freeman in 1950) and practically took over the Ramié family's factory, working intensely as a potter. In a charming Romanesque church at Vallauris there are two large murals by Picasso, *War* and *Peace,* dating from this period.

The artist's relations with Françoise Gilot ended in 1953; Olga Koklova, his wife, died in 1955. In 1954 Picasso met Jacqueline Roque, who was to become his second wife in 1958. In all the painter lived with a number of lovers, and two wives, but he had only four children: Paulo, whose mother was the ballerina Olga; Maïa, by Marie-Thérèse Walter; and Claude and Paloma, with Françoise Gilot. He had no descendants by his second lawful wife.

In 1957 Picasso began work on *Las Meninas* ("Maids of Honour"), which he exhibited at the Galerie Louise Leiris, Paris, in 1959. The 58 canvases making up the *Las Meninas* series were painted in little more than four months.

Portrait of Ramón Reventós, the Writer. *Watercolour, charcoal and pencil, Barcelona, 1899. (66.5 × 30.1 cm). P.M.B.*

Portrait of
Santiago Rusiñol
and Caricature of
Ramón Pitxot.
*Pen, ink and
aquatint,
Barcelona,
1890-1900.*
(32.2 × 22 cm).
P.M.B.

After attending a bullfight at Arles, the artist executed the 26 aquatints making up the series entitled *José Delgado's (Pepe Illo's) Tauromachy or the Art of Bullfighting.*

Picasso then bought the château at Vauvenargues and painted several canvases in which he seems to have been inspired by the surrounding landscape; he put them on exhibition in January 1963.

In June 1961 he had moved to Notre-Dame-de-Vie farmhouse, at Mougins, where he continued the series of pictures inspired by Manet's *Déjeuner sur l'herbe* ("Luncheon on the grass"), which had been commenced at Vauvenargues.

Between March and June 1963 Picasso painted over forty works comprising the series known as *The Painter and his Model.* He was then at the height of his creative fever, and went so far as to say that "Painting is stronger than me; it obliges me to do what it wants."

For this artist it was as if time stood still: he continued painting like a young man when he was over eighty years old, his inspiration astonishingly fresh, full of vivacity, dominating technical problems as always with the unique mastery of a genius.

In 1966 and 1967 Picasso untiringly produced drawings, as if he had a premonition that his end was near and wanted to leave to posterity as much graphic testimony of his genius as possible. In the words of Palau i Fabre, these were "drawings evincing a completely transformed Picasso; drawings in which the materials and techniques — pencil, crayon, ink, gouache — are combined and interchanged in the most unforeseeable ways, just as fantastic and realist

Portrait of Santiago Rusiñol. *Pen, ink and aquatint, Barcelona, 1899-1900. (10.3 × 9.2 cm). P.M.B.*

Portrait of Utrillo. *Pen, ink and gouache, Barcelona, 1899-1900. (7.8 × 8.5 cm). P.M.B.*

Portrait of Oriol Martí. *Pencil, pen and ink, Barcelona, 1899-1900. (16.6 × 11.3 cm). P.M.B.*

elements and the most diverse periods and personages are fused and mixed. In these drawings Picasso left far behind all the polemics about abstract and representational art, for each of the expressive elements employed brings with it a meaning, a substratum, which is in conflict with the others on the paper, the whole creating a world of suggestions going way beyond representation and the object represented.''

After Picasso had undergone a gall bladder operation in 1965, the following year a great exhibition in homage to the painter was organised in Paris: the Grand-Palais and the Petit-Palais presented an anthological collection of some 500 works, which was visited by over a million people.

Picasso's production from 1966 to 1970 totalled some 500 drawings, about 350 engravings, some 200 paintings and a large quantity of pottery.

An exhibition in which Picasso (by then 88 years old) put on show 140 paintings was inaugurated in the Popes' Palace in Avignon on May 1st 1970. The year after, when he was ninety, a number of his works were exhibited in the Louvre Museum. Picasso died at his Mougins residence on April 8th 1973.

Caricature of Joaquín Mir. *Pen, ink and watercolour. Barcelona, 1899-1900. (9 × 7.9 cm). P.M.B.*

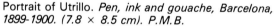

Printed menu of "Els Quatre Gats." *Barcelona, 1899-1900.*
(21.8 × 32.8 cm). P.M.B.

THE BLUE PERIOD

This phase of Picasso's work was characterised by the personal sadness and the melancholy surroundings of the world of figures, isolated from the banquet of life, that the painter portrayed in his canvases. As Pierre Daix wrote, however, "Picasso's plunge into the blue hell had nothing to do with self-pity, resignation or religion; on the contrary, it was the humanistic plunge of a man who contemplates his fellows, and shows them to us after having studied the spectacle himself. For this youth of twenty years of age went beyond his canvases, and if he was so humane it was because he succeeded in keeping his sanity, his independent spirit as a painter."

The part of Picasso's oeuvre known as the Blue Period was initiated in the autumn of 1901. His vigorous creative personality led him to diverge from the figurative style of painting prevalent at the time, conferring an independent, decidedly original character on his works. Picasso wrote to Max Jacob from Barcelona, referring to his "blue" painting: "The artists here find that there is too much soul, and not enough form, in my pictures: it is very funny." There was certainly a lot of soul in the artist's canvases of the Blue Period (which was to extend from autumn 1901 to late 1904); but there was also characteristic form which, shunning Impressionist techniques, expressed itself in a rigorous condensation of the images in compact blocks, always on a dull blue ground. Picasso lived alternately in Paris and Barcelona for the duration of the Blue Period, over three years. As Pierre Daix wrote in his biography of the painter, "He worked like a slave in both cities. This was the time that he lived in the greatest poverty, and was cold every winter." This is certainly a relevant detail, helping us to understand the genesis of the pictures Picasso painted in these years.

Of the works painted from 1901 to 1904 we should mention *Woman with sick Child,* a picture brimming with tenderness, painted in pastel on paper, kept in the Picasso Museum in Barcelona; *La Vie,* one of the best-known works of the Blue Period, oil on canvas, belonging to the Cleveland Museum of Art (in London there is a sketch in which the traits of the male figure in the foreground recall those of Picasso himself); *Celestine,* a work of extraordinary purity, oil on canvas, in a private collection in Paris; *The Pensive Harlequin,* oil on canvas, painted in 1901 but apparently not signed until 1927, which can be considered as corresponding to the transition to the Blue Period, now in the collection of the Metropolitan Museum of Art, New York; *The Old Guitarist,* oil on panel, of stylised lines, belonging to the Bartlett collection and

Study for the menu of "Els Quatre Gats." *Pen, ink and blurred conté crayon, Barcelona, 1899-1900. (46.7 × 30.8 cm). P.M.B.*

Mateu Fernández de Soto and a study for the menu of "Els Quatre Gats." *Pencil, pen and ink, Barcelona, 1899-1900. (32.1 × 22.7 cm). P.M.B.*

Sketch for the menu of "Els Quatre Gats." *Pencil, Barcelona, 1899-1900. (43 × 31 cm). P.M.B.*

Portrait of Jaime Sabartés, seated. *Watercolour and charcoal, Barcelona, 1899-1900. (50.5 × 33 cm). P.M.B.*

Portrait of Juan Vidal y Ventosa. *Charcoal and watercolour, Barcelona, 1899-1900. (47.6 × 27.6 cm). P.M.B.*

kept in the Art Institute of Chicago; *The Old Jew,* oil on canvas, of similar characteristics to the last-mentioned work, in the Pushkin State Museum of Fine Arts, Moscow; and *The Soler Family,* a charming composition in oil on canvas, kept in the Liège Museum.

THE ROSE PERIOD

The passage from the Blue Period to the Rose Period caused several changes in Picasso's aesthetics. The colours of his palette became lighter, and the vision of the world offered to us is also less sombre. There is a

Self-Portrait.
Pencil, Barcelona,
1899-1900.
(33.6 × 23.2 cm).
P.M.B.

Self-Portrait and sketch for the Caja de Previsión y Socorro poster. *Pencil and watercolour, Barcelona, 1899-1900. (22.3 × 32 cm). P.M.B.*

playful feeling in the Rose Period, in some way inherited from the Golden Age, so that Picasso's works overcame the hostile environment. His models were also different from those of the Blue Period. Alberto Martini wrote that the painter endeavoured to "strip his language of all symbolical implications, tending towards a limpid classicism of form, the lines moulded by exquisite profiles. From being the instrument expressing painful pathos, the composition now mov-

Study for the Caja de Previsión y Socorro poster. *Pencil, pen and ink, Barcelona, 1899-1900. (32.2 × 22.5 cm). P.M.B.*

The Artist's Sister Lola. *Pencil, Barcelona, 1899-1900. (48.4 × 32 cm). P.M.B.*

ed towards harmonious, elegant rhythms, subtly accompanied by a discreet commentary in colour; the artist had succeeded in calming his emotional violence for a while, and found notes of serenity and carefree gaiety in depicting the life of the circus, acrobats, jugglers, horsemen and tightrope walkers.'' The Rose Period began in the summer of 1904 and lasted until 1905. Picasso's aesthetical change coincided with his establishing his painting studio in the Bateau-Lavoir, in Rue Ravignan. This was the first time the artist had settled permanently in Paris and, as Pierre Daix observed, ''The correspondence between his new life and the modifications in his painting was not arbitrary. In Picasso the expression of his art is always related to the circumstances of his life, it is 'a way of keeping one's own diary,' as he said himself.'' His entry into contact with Gertrude Stein and her brother Leo, which occurred in this period, was a factor with a positive influence on his *modus vivendi:* the two North Americans were persons with a solid financial position and through them, Picasso was able to sell his works for substantial quantities of money, for the first time in his life.

The stylistic transformation in Picasso's oeuvre corresponding to the Rose Period was initiated with *The Actor,* an oil painting on canvas executed in the winter of 1904, now in the Metropolitan Museum of Art, New York; and concluded with *Family of Saltimbanques,* a large oil painting on canvas, dated 1905, belonging to the Dale Collection and kept in the National Gallery at Washington. This very beautiful picture is with justice considered to be the masterpiece of the Rose Period. It depicts a family of travelling acrobats resting on their journey. The six figures are depicted with singular poetic mastery: a heavily-built clown, no longer young, painted in red; a harlequin with a romantic appearance, wearing a costume adorned with multicoloured triangles; an adolescent

Seated Woman with Shawl. *Charcoal and pastel on glazed paper, Barcelona, 1899-1900. (23 × 26 cm). P.M.B.*

Sketch. *Pastel, Paris, 1900.*
(10.5 × 6 cm). P.M.B.

Sketch. *Pencil, watercolour and pastel,*
Barcelona, 1900. (10.5 × 6 cm). P.M.B.

Sketch. *Pastel, Paris, 1900.*
(10.5 × 6 cm). P.M.B.

with slender hips; two children; and a beautiful young woman wearing a red skirt and a broad yellow straw hat adorned with red flowers. The atmosphere is impregnated with delicate pink tones. The whole is balanced, serene, elegantly beautiful. The composition and colour make up an artistic ensemble full of rhythm.

Other characteristic works of the Rose Period include *The Three Dutch Girls,* gouache on paper, painted in Schoorldam, where Picasso spent a month in 1905, belonging to the National Museum of Modern Art, Paris; *Youth crowned with Flowers,* oil on canvas, which began as a simple portrait of a young worker but was later modified by the artist, in the Whitney collection (New York); *The Two Brothers,* oil on can-vas, displaying archaic simplicity and intense colours in the background, exhibited (on loan from the Staechelin Foundation) at the Kunstmuseum in Basle; *Boy Leading a Horse,* a work of fine, lyrical col-ours counterpointed by the vigour of the forms, in the Paley collection (New York); *Nude: Fernande Olivier,* which recalls figures of primitive Iberian art, in the Zacks collection (Toronto); *Self-Portrait as Harlequin in a Café,* an intensely coloured oil painting on can-vas, set in the "Lapin agile" cabaret in Montmartre — the proprietor appears in the background of the pic-ture, playing a guitar — in the Payson collection (New York); and *Clown and small Acrobat,* charcoal, pastel and watercolour on paper, in the Baltimore Museum of Art.

The Embrace. *Pastel,
Paris, 1900.
(59 × 35 cm). P.M.B.*

In the Dressing Room. *Pastel, Paris, 1900.*
(48 × 53 cm). P.M.B.

Girl in White by a Window (Lola in the Studio in Calle Riera de San Juan). *Oil on canvas, Barcelona, 1900. (55.5 × 46 cm). P.M.B.*

Window. *Oil on canvas, Paris, 1900. (50 × 32.5 cm). P.M.B.*

GOSOL, A NEW ADVENTURE FOR PICASSO

Towards the late summer and early autumn of 1906, Picasso made a daring excursion along an aesthetic path that greatly enriched his artistic production. In the words of Alberto Martini, ''With the powerfulness and the elementary forms of Catalan Romanesque architecture and, in particular, of pre-Roman Iberian sculpture before his eyes, he suddenly turned to an abrupt formal construction of the image, structuring it with monumental dimensions in no way conforming to classical proportions.''

The *Portrait of Gertrude Stein* — begun in Paris in the winter of 1905-1906 and altered when the painter returned from Gósol — is considered to be the first work of this new period in Picasso's production. When it was suggested to the North American writer that the portrait was not in her likeness, she rejected the criticism and affirmed that ''the only image of me which will always be me'' was precisely the portrait painted by Picasso.

Drawing for the magazine
''Joventut'' (''Youth'').
*Pen and ink, on lined
paper, Barcelona, 1900.
(13.4 × 17.4 cm).
P.M.B.*

Study for illustration for
''El Clam de les Verges''
(''The Virgins' Cry'').
*Pencil, Barcelona, 1900.
(32 × 22 cm). P.M.B.*

Self-Portrait *(sketches of
Oriol Martí, Pompeu
Gener and other figures).
Pencil, pen and ink,
Barcelona, 1900.
(32 × 22 cm). P.M.B.*

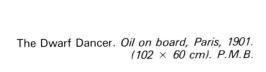

Waiting (Margot). *Oil on board, Paris, 1901.*
(69.5 × 57 cm). P.M.B.

While Picasso was in Gósol his painting underwent an intense process of definition. Pierre Daix wrote that, "In the privileged, chosen face of Gertrude Stein, or in his own, Picasso offers us an in-depth reading. He breaks with the appearance so as to remain faithful to the volumes, but he contrives to elude abstraction, generalisation or inexpressiveness in the pure volume. He rejects the details so as to preserve the attitude and characteristic air of the model, the way he or she is, in fact."

Another canvas characteristic of this period of return to the painter's roots — an interlude between the Rose Period and the pre-Cubism reflected in *Les Demoiselles d'Avignon* — is the *Self-Portrait with a Palette* created in Paris in autumn 1906, kept in the Philadelphia Museum of Art (A.E. Gallatin Collection). The figure is impregnated with a primitive air and depicted in balanced planes highlighting the volumes. There is nothing anecdotal in this *Self-Portrait,* no accessories to hinder one's vision of the work or to reduce its vigour.

Picasso painted several works during this period at Gósol, among them *Reclining Nude, Woman with Headscarf, Nude with Hair, Nude with Hands Together,* and *Two Nudes.* All these paintings are connected by an obvious stylistic relationship and their aesthetics correspond to the process of definition pursued by Picasso in 1906. As Daix noted, this definition meant "venturing into a field where all similarity with the conventional abstract appearance is negated, excluded."

The Dwarf Dancer. *Oil on board, Paris, 1901.*
(102 × 60 cm). P.M.B.

The End of the
Act. *Pastel on
canvas, Paris,
1900-01.
(72 × 46 cm).
P.M.B.*

PICASSO'S CUBISM

Picasso, who was already an extraordinary artist at the age of twenty, constantly excelled himself with the passage of time, until he surpassed all the boundaries of universal plastic arts and established himself as the firm rival of the greatest artists of all time. There is always an element of magic in his protean oeuvre: Picasso was the greatest thaumaturge of 20th-century art. He invaded all fields of art and explored them in depth, making them his own and enriching them with his highly personal contribution. Picasso's Cubist phase began after the long, arduous struggle of investigation represented by his painting *Les Demoiselles d'Avignon* (now in the Museum of Modern Art, New York). As Alberto Martini wrote, "Originally the subject was to be a group of prostitutes — in Barcelona there was indeed a brothel in Carrer Aviñó — eating in the company of a sailor and a student meditating on a skull: a subject, thus, still within the poetic climate of symbolism — despite coming after the ruptures caused by the works of the Rose Period and the phase of transition — with allusions to the themes of eroticism, death and escape. During the production of the work, the subject was not only radically transformed to the point that it lost all symbolic implications, but it was also entirely destroyed by the interest applied to the object, that is, to the picture as a reality and as an image independent of the appearance of things, of purely visual perception." In the process of elaboration of this pre-Cubist work, Picasso's observation that "I try to paint what I have found, not what I am looking for" was completely fulfilled. What Picasso had found on this occasion was the aesthetic path that was to lead him directly to Cubism. When the artist from Málaga

Rastaquouères. *Watercolour, pen and ink, Paris, 1901. (18 × 11.5 cm). P.M.B.*

Nude Woman, reclining, with the Artist at her feet.
*Watercolour, pen and ink, Barcelona, 1901.
(17.6 × 23.2 cm). P.M.B.*

Two Nude Women. *Coloured crayons, pen and ink on
card (pasteboard), Barcelona, 1901. (9 × 13.3 cm).
P.M.B.*

broke reality up into planes, a whole new aesthetic
conception was opened up to him.

The atmosphere generated around the painter as a
result of his aesthetic research while he was working
on *Les Demoiselles d'Avignon* finally constituted the
inspiration that imposed the painting on Picasso. The
artist had intended to paint one thing, but which
subsequently turned out to be radically different. It
seems that the work was going to be entitled *The
Avignon Brothel* but when it was finished, in 1907,
André Salmon, poet and Picasso's friend, gave it the
name *Les Demoiselles d'Avignon,* by which it is now
universally known.

In this canvas Picasso broke with all the conventional
models of painting as practised up to that time. In the
words of Pierre Daix, ''The rupture with the fixity in
space and time of classical perspective was total. It is
this contrast between the continuity of the outline
and the discontinuity of the different aspects that pro-
vokes the 'deformations.' *Les Demoiselles d'Avignon*
affirms the reality of this problem neglected by the
Renaissance: that sight, the persistence of impres-
sions from the retina, and the training of vision by experience make us perceive, in a way — or conceive —
the back, the reverse, of objects and beings. To
Velazquéz' mirror, to Caravaggio's light, Picasso insisted on opposing the forms themselves, volumes independent of the plane, as also the nature of the
light.''

This was a unique phenomenon. Such daring in art
could not be tolerated. Picasso's irreverence, in
rebellion against the demands of Renaissance norms
until then religiously observed, outraged the world.
Viewers of *Les Demoiselles d'Avignon* felt
disconcerted and enraged. Picasso, however, was to
go further, with Cubism and after Cubism. His
creative and inventive capacity was practically inter-
minable, and was to astonish experts and the

Still Life. *Oil on canvas, Paris, 1901. (59 × 78 cm).*
P.M.B.

uninitiated in the years to come. Cubism was even debated as a subject of law and order in the Chamber of Deputies in Paris, in the session of December 3rd 1912, in the course of which M. Jules-Louis Breton asked the Under-Secretary of State ''What measures he was prepared to take to avoid a repetition of the artistic scandal occasioned by the last Salon d'Automne.''

Picasso's contribution to Cubism was paramount. Cézanne's painting played an important part in his transition to the Cubist experience. Pierre Daix wrote that ''The point of view, obviously a theme in Cézanne's perspective, dominates objects the better to discover them; but Picasso augmented the break with classical perspective, paying more attention to the interplay between forms, using the effect of refraction in the transparency of a glass, or the sections of a funnel above some cups, to highlight this.''

From 1909 to 1912, Picasso's Cubism was characterised by objective representation of reality, based on the painter's intellectual acquaintance with it. This was the period of Analytical Cubism, which gave way from 1912 to 1916 to a phase in which the artistic depiction of reality was articulated in a complex way, the artist relying on the relations evoked by the subject in his mind, psychology and memory. This second Cubist stage in Picasso, freer and more spontaneous than the first, is known as Synthetic Cubism. Picasso always demanded absolute freedom in his artistic expression. He was incapable of submitting to any aesthetic dogma. "Cubism," said the painter himself, "is no different from other schools in paint-

Self-Portrait. *Watercolour, pen and ink, Barcelona, 1901. (20.7 × 13.1 cm). P.M.B.*

Portrait of Joaquín Mir. *Pencil and watercolour, Barcelona, 1901. (20.8 × 15.5 cm). P.M.B.*

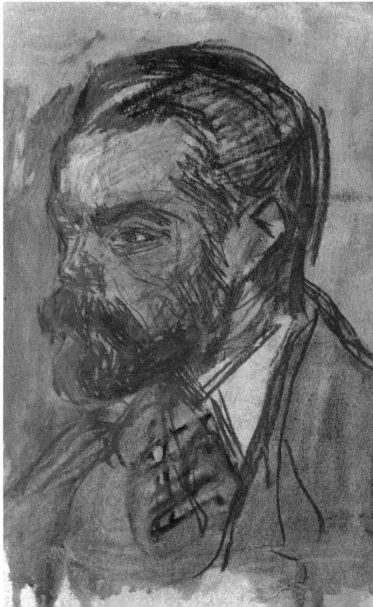

Rooftops in Barcelona. *Oil on canvas, Barcelona, 1902. (57.8 × 60.3 cm). P.M.B.*

Portrait of Sebastián Junyent. *Oil on canvas, Barcelona, 1902. (73 × 60 cm). P.M.B.*

ing. They all have in common the same principles and elements. The fact that Cubism has for a long time not been understood (...) does not mean that it has no value. The fact that I don't read German, because pages written in that language are just black on white for me, does not mean that the German language does not exist either; nor do I blame the author of the pages, rather I blame myself. (...) Cubism is not a seed, nor an art in gestation, but a phase of primary forms, and these forms put into effect have the right to live their own existence. (...) People have tried to explain Cubism by means of mathematics, geometry, trigonometry, chemistry, psychoanalysis, music, and I don't know how many other things. All that is pure literature. For us Cubism is no more than a way of expressing what our eyes and our minds perceive, with all the possibilities that drawing and colour contain in their own qualities. In it we find a source of unexpected pleasure, of discoveries.'' It is thus perfectly clear that Picasso always felt himself to be a painter and only a painter, including in his Cubist phase. He stated that, ''I have always painted for my age; I have never been troubled by the spirit of search. I express what I see, sometimes in different ways. I neither lay down rules nor carry out experiments. When I have something to say, I say it in the manner I think I should. There is no transition art; there are simply better and worse artists.''

Among Picasso's Cubist works, mention may be made of *Still Life* (Kunstmuseum, Basle), painted with influences from Cézanne in 1908, which constitutes an example of the artist's first steps in the field of Cubism; *The Guitarist* (oil on canvas, 1910, National Museum of Modern Art, Paris); *Bottle of Bass* (oil on canvas, 1912, Beyeler Gallery, Basle); *The Aficionado,* painted at Sorgues in 1912, depicting the newspaper ''El Torero'' and a banderilla on a small table (Kunstmuseum, Basle); Le Vieux Marc, oil on canvas, 1912-1913, in the National Museum of Modern Art, Paris; *Woman in a Chemise, Seated in an Armchair* (1913, L. Pudelko Eichmann Collection,

La Mujer del Mechón. *Watercolour, Barcelona, 1903. (50 × 37 cm). P.M.B.*

Portrait of Sebastián Junyer. *Oil on paper, Barcelona, 1902-03. (56 × 46 cm). P.M.B.*

Florence), considered to be one of the masterpieces of Cubism; *The Violin* (oil on canvas, 1913, Siegfried Rosengart Collection, Lucerne), a characteristic work of Picasso's Synthetic Cubism period, showing a firm tendency to objectivity, with *papiers collés* (''pasted papers'') on the canvas; *Verre, Bouteille de Vin, Journal sur une Table* (collage and drawing, dated 1914, Jean Dalsace Collection, Paris); *Purgative (papiers collés,* gouache and charcoal, 1914, Jeanne Bucher Gallery, Paris); and *Guitar, Skull and Newspaper* (oil on canvas, 1914, C.M.H. Bergruen Collection, Paris).

PICASSO AND SURREALISM

The genius from Málaga was not impervious to any of the avant-garde movements that occurred in the protracted course of his life: an artist of his infinite creative capacity could not be. The very nature of Picasso's authenticity, however, prevented his absolute adherence to a particular aesthetic trend, his submission to more or less dogmatic theoretical propositions or artistic creeds. He extracted here and there whatever he considered useful and necessary to

Maternity. *Pastel and charcoal, Barcelona, 1903. (46 × 40 cm). P.M.B.*

The Madman. *Watercolour, Paris, 1904. (85 × 35 cm).
P.M.B.*

express himself as forthrightly and as persuasively as possible. He assimilated the innovatory elements created by others in the plastic arts and personalised them in order to vivify and renovate his own oeuvre. It is true that, as Alberto Martini observed, Picasso ''received a considerable number of ideas from the contemporary Surrealist researches, especially through his regular contacts with Eluard and Breton; but this was a reciprocal relationship, for the Surrealist painters precisely, especially Max Ernst and Miró, obtained great benefits from Picasso's oeuvre. For the Spanish painter, Surrealism was a stimulus to liberate his thought from traditional cognitive structures — an effort that, with felicitous intuition, he had already initiated in pre-War years (...); it was a spur to the exploration of his inner world, of the secret heritage of the subconscious in both its private and collective sectors. Picasso gave the Surrealists a lesson in language and important precepts regarding the free orchestration of art forms following one's mental structuring of reality, in the awareness that the only realities one possesses are those residing in one's interior, whereas all that is outside can only be perceived by means of a representational process which, in the case of Picasso, was not applied to the appearance of things, but to their mental and emotional function.'' This is a long quotation, but it offers the advantage of explaining with all clarity the nature of the painter's relations with the Surrealist creative process. Breton himself, furthermore, acknowledged Surrealism's indebtedness to the artist from Málaga when he stated that, without Picasso's artistic researches, the Surrealists' position ''could have been delayed or lost.'' One cannot, strictly speaking, refer to a Surrealist Picasso. The painter was at all stages

The Frugal Repast. *Etching, Paris, 1904. (50.9 × 41 cm).
P.M.B.*

outside the movement led by André Breton. He coincided with the Surrealists in certain aspects related to the genesis of the creative process, but he never followed Breton's canons, rather those dictated by his own sensitivity, which was too rich to be submitted to others' impositions. In the words of Pierre Daix, ''Picasso, like the younger members of the Surrealist movement, was fighting against an intolerable, unacceptable reality; at the precise time when he felt more than ever the attractions of beauty, the desire to sing to his wife, his son and all the pleasures of the world. With this background, it is absurd to try to oppose reconciliation with reality and escape, or logic and monsters. They coexisted in Picasso, as in Paul Eluard (who was to depart for Polynesia) and in the Surrealist movement itself, which was not to be dispersed until later on. Picasso's interlocutors were gradually changed. Gauguin and Douanier Rousseau were succeeded by Poussin and Ingres, Iberian and Negro influences by Mycenaean impulses and Hieronymus Bosch's dreams. All this, however, within the continuity both of his oeuvre and of his relations with the precursors, in the unity of a painter who did not disperse or back down, although he corrected, reproved and criticised himself relentlessly.''
A vigorously playful feeling — ubiquitous, with greater or lesser intensity, in Picasso's oeuvre — influenced the painter at the time when he felt attracted by the expressive freedom characterising Surrealism. Nor should it be forgotten that he had been extending the fields of his vast artistic adventure in such a way that when the Surrealist movement appeared, the intensity with which he had been working throughout

Portrait of Mme Canals. *Oil on canvas, Paris, 1905.*
(88 × 68 cm). P.M.B.

the first quarter of the 20th century had almost exhausted the means of expression that he used. At this stage the painter appropriated a new instrument to facilitate his artistic creation: the interior monologue, which coincided with what is considered as Picasso's Surrealist facet.

The *Surrealist Manifesto* was made public in 1924; among the painters that "could be considered Surrealists" it cited Uccello, Seurat, Moreau, Matisse, Derain, Picasso, Braque, Duchamp, Picabia, Chirico, Klee, Man Ray, Max Ernst and Masson. According to J. Pierre, Picasso was the first contemporary artist who, in order to clarify the concept of the "interior model," quoted *Le Surréalisme et la Peinture* (a study by André Breton published as a book in 1928 but previously printed in *La Révolution Surréaliste,* a magazine that lasted from 1924 to 1929, directed first by Naville and Péret and later, from issue 4 onwards, by Breton himself); and also the first to "find the real reason for painting." "That the position held by us now could have been delayed or lost depended only on a failure in the determination of this man." "This unequivocally underlines the repercussion of Picasso's Cubism on the whole of Surrealism, a fact which to this day surprises some art historians, for whom Cézanne's work is the only thing that can explain the Cubist phenomenon."

Works by Picasso that are generally considered Surrealist include *The Three Dancers* (1925; in 1965 it was still in the artist's private collection), a painting corresponding to the aesthetics of the "interior monologue"; *Still Life with Antique Head* (1925, National Museum of Modern Art, Paris); *The Studio* (1927-1928, Museum of Modern Art, New York); *Seated Bather* (1930, Museum of Modern Art, New York); *Girl Before a Mirror* (1932, Museum of Modern Art, New York); and *The Muse* (1935, National Museum of Modern Art, Paris) — all brilliant canvases.

La salchichona (Woman with Mantilla). *Oil on canvas, Barcelona, 1917. (116 × 89 cm). P.M.B.*

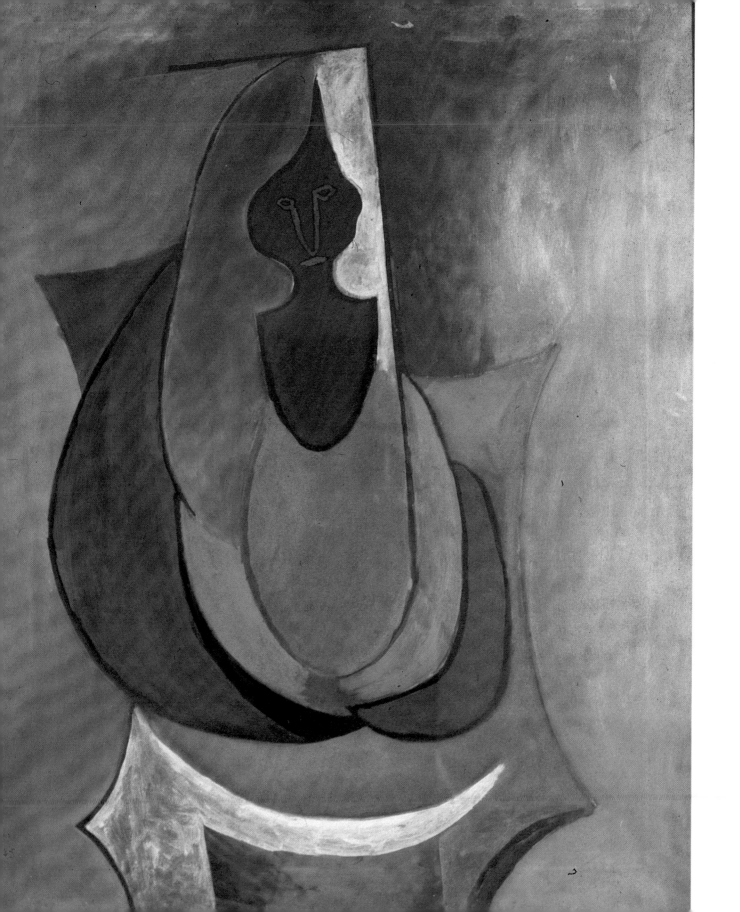

Cubist figure. *Oil on canvas, Barcelona, 1917. (116 × 89.2 cm). P.M.B.*

Fruit Bowl. *Oil on canvas, Barcelona, 1917. (40 × 28.1 cm). P.M.B.*

Figure in an Armchair. *Oil on canvas, Barcelona, 1917. (92 × 64.4 cm). P.M.B.*

Blanquita Suárez. *Oil on canvas, Barcelona, 1917. (73.3 × 47 cm). P.M.B.*

PICASSO'S REINTERPRETATIONS OF PICTORIAL MYTHS

In 1953 Picasso painted a series of works to which he dedicated unusual vehemence. It would seem as if the artist felt ill-at-ease with himself and that this sensation, this internal conflict, is reflected in his oeuvre. Paintings such as *Head of Reclining Woman, Bust of Woman, Woman Seated, Woman and Dog on a Blue Ground* and *Woman with Hat* date from 1953. These are works in which the painter seems to have taken pleasure in demonstrating his cruelty by means of his brushes.

The portrait of Stalin, executed for *Lettres Françaises* (a magazine at that time directed by the Communist poet Louis Aragon), also dates from 1953. Picasso based it on a photograph and, as Pierre Daix wrote, "The portrait of Stalin as a young man that he sent was in the style of his portraits of Beloyannis and Henri Martin. Its publication had the effect of a bomb shell. Picasso was attacked both by those who saw in the portrait an offence against the memory of Stalin

Figure with Fruit
Bowl. *Oil on
canvas, Barcelona,
1917.
(100 × 70.2 cm).*
P.M.B.

Sabartés as a Gentleman of Philip II's time. *Pencil, Paris, 1938. (29 × 21 cm). P.M.B.*

Portrait of Sabartés with a Ruff. *Pencil, Paris, 1938. (36 × 27 cm). P.M.B.*

Portrait of Jaime Sabartés in a Monk's Habit. *Pencil, Paris, 1938. (36 × 27 cm). P.M.B.*

and by those who considered the Russian's death a happy event. Although Maurice Thorez' return to France, in mid-March, put an end to the Communist Party's attacks on Picasso and Aragon, this spring was a time of great isolation for the former.''

We should recall that Picasso had been considered a luxury and an honour for the French Communists. The artist limited his comments on the incident to a certain pique: ''I took my bunch of flowers to the burial. They didn't like it. These things happen; but one doesn't ordinarily insult people coarsely because one doesn't like their flowers.''

The French Communists protested because Picasso depicted Stalin with a cruel look; but can anyone question his cruelty? Nor did they appreciate the fact that the painter represented him as of an Asiatic ethnic type. Picasso shrugged off the Communists' reproaches and commented to Pierre Daix that he had thought of adding a wreath of flowers on Stalin's head, adding, ''But it would have been the same. Everything would have been identical. They wouldn't have put up with that either. I also thought of drawing him nude. Heroes are always naked. Can you imagine, if I had drawn him absolutely naked…? That's the way it is; but you'll see'' — he concluded caustically — ''later on, they'll use my drawing to illustrate articles in the dictionary.''

After the crisis of 1953, a year in which he was harshly

Minotauromachy. *Etching, Paris, 1935. (49.8 × 69.3 cm).*
P.M.B.

criticised from all sides, Picasso once again impulsed his artistic inspiration and launched himself along a hitherto unexplored path of creation. From 1954 to 1960, he carried out a series of momentous exercises based on *Women of Algiers,* a painting by Delacroix; *Las Meninas* (''Maids of Honour'') by Velázquez; and *Déjeuner sur l'herbe* (''Luncheon on the Grass'') by Manet. In these original artistic experiments Picasso undertook the daring enterprise of showing the reverse of great pictorial myths. They were like impas-

sioned dialectical debates between Picasso, on one hand, and Delacroix, Velázquez and Manet, successively, on the other: of crucial interest for understanding the genesis of artistic creation. Delacroix painted *Women of Algiers* in 1834; later, in 1849, he produced a new version, omitting the rose displayed by one of the women in the earlier painting. Picasso based himself on Delacroix's painting, and also took into account Matisse's canvas entitled *Odalisques,* in the execution of his interesting ex-

Flower-vase. *Gouache, Paris, 1943. (65 × 49.5 cm).*
P.M.B.

periments on the subject, showing its other side. Commenting on his own series on *Women of Algiers,* the painter remarked to Penrose: ''When Matisse died he left his odalisques to me as a legacy.'' Earlier, in 1932, Picasso had said: ''In the end, it all depends on oneself. It is a sun, with thousands of rays, inside one. The rest is nothing. For that reason alone Matisse is Matisse, for example — because he has that sun inside him.''

The same inquisitive impulse drove Picasso to his dialectical confrontation with Velázquez; their artistic dialogue was developed in *Las Meninas.* The resultant series of works now enriches the Picasso Museum in Barcelona. Alberto Martini wrote that, ''In *Las Meninas* there are already indications of a theme that, in more recent years, became an obsession for Picasso: the relationship between the artist and the model. Velázquez, as a good realist, avoided the ar-

Composition with Flower Vase. *Colour lithograph, Paris, 1947. (45 × 60 cm). P.M.B.*

Centaur playing Pipes. *Etching,*
1948. (32 × 25 cm). P.M.B.

Dying Centaur. *Etching, 1948. (32 × 25 cm).*
P.M.B.

Centaur and Waggon. *Etching,*
1948. (37 × 25 cm). P.M.B.

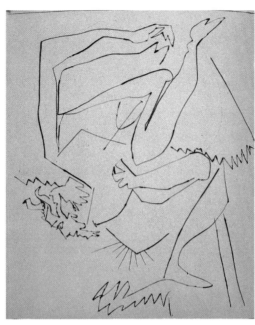

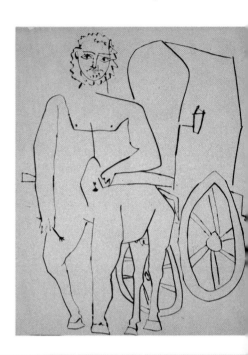

Scenes of the Birth of a Centaur. *Etching, 1948.*
(33 × 25 cm). P.M.B.

bitrariness of simultaneously depicting his own person and the models (the royal family) in this canvas; ingeniously, he represented them by means of a mirror reflecting their figures (notwithstanding, he also rejected the arbitrariness of representing himself and the scene he was painting from his models' point of view). Picasso, whose realism had broken the chains of the outward appearance, did not resort to the subtle device of the mirror; to prove to himself that any given object is an entity belonging to the field of thought, not the appearance of reality, he painted his person directly opposite the model, almost always a woman, demonstrating the distance separating the external appearance of the real object and the painted image.'' Picasso's *Las Meninas* series stressed, once

The Dove. *Lithograph, 1949. (54.5 × 70 cm). P.M.B.*

again, that the great painter dominated all the means of modern painting techniques. Under the impulse of his (never refuted) playful nature, he played with the motifs and — in the same way as children with their toys — drew their guts out into the open air, achieving charmingly original effects. The *Las Meninas* series, painted in 1957, constitutes one of the most surprising, novel successes of modern painting.

In 1960 Picasso repeated the artistic interplay he had initiated with Delacroix and continued with Velázquez, painting his *Déjeuner sur l'herbe* (in the artist's collection in 1971), the start of the cycle inspired by Manet's famous painting. The following year he executed another canvas with the same title (in the Rosengart Collection, Lucerne); in total there were to be some twenty-five variations, not counting the numerous preparatory drawings and sketches. The composition of the figures in this series is more com-

The Dove. *Lithograph, 1947. (27 × 45 cm). P.M.B.*

plex and more obscure than in *Women of Algiers* and *Las Meninas.*

In the words of Pierre Daix, ''Manet was an old companion in Picasso's dreams and this first series (the drawings inspired by Manet's picture executed at Vauvenargues in early August 1959) evinces the freedom of 'discussions between accomplices.' The black and white drawings, as also the two in colour, have in common the emphasis with which they treat a figure to which Manet had also given considerable importance: that of the woman wearing a shirt, bathing her feet in the river. Picasso, however, takes her, appropriates her, shows her naked.'' The artist was to recur to this image several times, for example in *Woman in Chemise* and *Woman bathing her feet.*

PICASSO THE ENGRAVER

Pablo Picasso's unique artistic personality was not limited to painting; far from it. There was also Picasso the engraver, Picasso the potter, and Picasso the sculptor, of undeniably extraordinary quality and importance within each of these facets of artistic creation.

Picasso's graphic work would alone be sufficient for the artist to figure in art history as one of the great figures of universal creation. In the course of his life — longer and more fertile than most — Picasso engraved a large quantity of magnificent works on the most diverse subjects: mythology, tauromachy, the figures of his different wives and lovers, erotic themes, Spanish Golden Age subjects, book illustrations... The artist used the most varied techniques, working linoleum, copper, stone, wood and celluloid with burin, pen, brush or thick pencil. Etchings,

Seated Woman, in Profile. *Etching (cancelled print), 1951. (14 × 10 cm). P.M.B.*

The Corrida. *Pastel and gouache on canvas, Barcelona, 1900. (16.2 × 30.5 cm). Cau Ferrat Museum, Sitges.*

aquatints or dry-points — all Picasso's graphic works bear the stamp of his ummistakable style.

The brilliant painter felt strongly attracted to engraving from a youthful age; he worked untiringly as an engraver. He produced some 350 engravings in the space of little more than 6 months, in 1968, at his studio at Mougins. On his death, he bequeathed to mankind a body of engravings comparable with those of Dürer, Rembrandt or Goya. Picasso made a decisive contribution to the great revolution in engraving techniques of the modern age. He practised all these techniques in collaboration with the greatest craftsmen of the time and attained absolute mastery of all their expressive mechanisms and technical secrets. In his engravings as in his paintings, one can observe that Picasso constantly renovated his art. His insatiable curiosity and unlimited creative capacity can also be noted in his graphic work, putting Picasso at the head of the engravers of the 20th century.

The artist's unrivalled genius — genius not far removed from magic — as a draughtsman was manifest whenever he engraved. As a result, Picasso's engravings were always not only perfectly resolved as regards their technique, but at the same time dynamic works, constantly vital, endowed with the charm of the painter's creative genius.

Picasso is said to have been the author of more than 2,200 works in the field of engraving and prints. This high number of original works bears testimony to the marvellous creative capacity of this monster (there is no other term that better defines Picasso's genius) of 20th-century art.

In his work as an engraver, just as in his painting, Picasso rejected all rhetoric and concentrated on the themes of life, taking his inspiration from motifs closely linked with the human condition. Myth, with all the human implications of the corresponding fables, is often represented in Picasso's engravings, as for example in those entitled *Monster con-*

templated by four Children (dated 1933), *The Minotaur's Orgy* (from the same year), *Seated Girl contemplating the Minotaur* (also 1933) and *Blind Minotaur* (1935). Pierre Daix wrote that "The minotaur embodied a new degree of freedom for Picasso in relation to the limitations that his own researches had set."

The painter was familiar with the tecniques of woodcut and monotype as early as in 1899, when he engraved *El Zurdo; The Frugal Repast* dates from 1904. Later, in 1919, he took to lithography. He started to use the aquatint process in 1934, and in 1939 he executed his first linocuts. One can see that there was no haste in Picasso's training as an engraver; which is far from meaning that he did not work intensely, as an artist avid for new goals, in this facet.

The outstanding plates in Picasso's engraving oeuvre include those making up the *Saltimbanques* series, created in 1913; Balzac's *Le Chef d'oeuvre inconnu*

Suerte de varas ("Wounding Bull with Lance"). *Etching (cancelled print), 1957. (20 × 30 cm). P.M.B.*

Bullfighting at Vallauris. *Linocut in colour, Vallauris, 1955. (66.5 × 52 cm). P.M.B.*

Bulls in the Country. *Etching, 1957. (20 × 30 cm). P.M.B.*

Landscape. *Oil on canvas, Cannes, 1957. (16 × 22 cm).*
P.M.B.

Les Pigeons. *Oil on canvas, Cannes, 1957.*
(100 × 80 cm). P.M.B.

("The Unknown Masterpiece"), executed in 1927 and published in 1931, as also Ovid's *Metamorphoses;* the *Vollard Suite,* comprising engravings carried out from 1927 to 1937; *Poems and Lithographs* (1949); and *Pepe Illo's Tauromachy or the Art of Bullfighting,* a series published by Gustavo Gili in Barcelona in 1959. There are other important engravings by Picasso related to such themes as women and love, the artist and his model, death, the pleasures of life, and erotic motifs — all treated with unsurpassable, picaresque expressive charm and marvellous technical control.

PICASSO AS A POTTER

Picasso was always miraculously young in human and artistic terms; in 1947, at sixty-six years of age, he began to learn a new art — pottery. The previous year the painter had returned to Vallauris in search of an old potter he had met with Paul Eluard years earlier, before the war had broken out. Suzanne and Georges Ramié had had to close the kilns one after another and were trying to modernise the production of ceramic pieces; they had installed an electric kiln.

Portrait of Jacqueline. *Oil on canvas, Cannes, 1957.*
(116 × 89 cm). P.M.B.

One afternoon in August 1947, as Georges Ramié himself wrote, Picasso "went to Golfe Juan, to the house of Fort, an engraver friend of his. He could very well have gone to the beach that day, or visited other friends, or stayed in his studio to work in the silent calm that was always so favourable to him. But he no doubt felt, in an obscure corner of his subconscious, that the right time to fulfil a part of his destiny had come. People were already talking, with great interest, of the potters' exhibition at Vallauris; always keen to be acquainted with things, Picasso gave in to the desire to visit it."

The artist was profoundly attracted by the pieces on show. The rebirth of the pottery tradition at Vallauris was due largely to him. Since he first sat at the potter's wheel to mould pieces, Picasso did not stop: he advanced, just as he had in other fields, with great enthusiasm and constant dedication, until he became consummate in the craft. He grew to love the mysterious material — as Ramié called the mass moulded by potters — that shows itself "so sensitive to the finger that violates it," but which reacts "with such rigour to the slightest variations in humidity; so untractable for those who confront it without understanding it, but so submissive to those who treat it with respect; so fragile when it is moulded, as if surprised by its prior metamorphosis, but which has yet to be purified by the horrors of fire, to come out of it incombustible and breakable. (...) There were more than enough attractive qualities and redoubtable risks to tempt Picasso's adventurous spirit."

The artist of genius liked this malleable material, which seemed to take on an almost human sensitivity by contact with the fingers caressing it. Picasso's magic fingers drew fascinatingly, originally beautiful forms out of the clay, which was in turn generous, grateful to be treated with love by these hands, so expert in artistic and amorous activities. For Picasso, his aptitude as a potter was an astonishing discovery. He

had never considered pottery a minor art; in the words of Pierre Daix, ''All his work up to 1947 shows that pre-Hellenic and Greek pottery, as also the ceramics of American civilisations, were the subject of his consideration and study.'' Until 1947, however, he saw ceramic pieces with sympathy, if not with decided admiration, but from the outside, as a spectator enjoying them in his sensitivity; but then, when he too was a potter, he saw the grandeur and the possibilities of this ancient art from the inside, as an artist enjoying the pleasure of creating his own works Pottery was never a mere distraction for Picasso, but

Las Meninas (''Maids of Honour''). *Oil on canvas, Cannes, 1957. (194 × 260 cm). P.M.B.*

Las Meninas *(the whole). Oil on canvas, Cannes, 1957.*
(129 × 161 cm). P.M.B.

an artistic occupation to which, as in all his creative facets, he dedicated all the capacity of his spirit. Georges Ramié said that he gained control of ''the spirit of fire that has fascinated mankind from time immemorial, causing men to keep it in captivity in their hearths. Reference has so often been made to Picasso's penetrating gaze that it should indeed be said that he has invincible eyes, capable of resisting

— while watching over the kiln — the bright shaft of the flame glowing with unbearable white light at over a thousand degrees.''

In what may be considered as Picasso's first phase as a potter he produced splendid plates and other pieces in traditional forms. He did not diverge far from the traditions in pottery of Greece, Mycenae or Vallauris itself in this period, but one can detect in these early

Las Meninas. *Oil on canvas, Cannes, 1957.*
(129 × 161 cm). P.M.B.

pieces a certain creative tension driving him towards untrodden paths. As Pierre Daix observed, ''Picasso practised all technical modes, took them to their final extremes, and turned the failures, the accidents and the unforeseen results to his advantage, as always; but in pottery one never knows if a piece will resist the kiln, nor how the glaze will turn out. The results were fascinating, especially for anyone concerned to cap-

ture Picasso's struggles with the material he used. In his new activity he manipulated utilitarian forms — bowls, plates, vases — to combine them with the ideas suggested by the said forms: thence the sun-bowls, the bullring-bowls, the clay vases, the vases as heads. Even the technical exercises were executed with such agility that they seem natural: the vase as a statuette of a woman supporting another smaller vase in its arm/handle, the vases in the form of a kneeling woman — these are marvels of simplicity.''

Picasso rapidly mastered the techniques of pottery and indulged himself, applying the most unusual, enchanting forms in his ceramic pieces. In his second phase as a potter one can observe his preoccupation to endow the volumes with relief. Sometimes the forms even occur spontaneously, although always fascinating, subordinated to the hierarchical values of the volume. Ramié stated that these were ''compositions with very rigorous style and architecture, although sometimes quite laborious to produce: con-ical ensembles with off-centre eyes, structures made up of purposeless elements, bundles of dislocated forms. All the facilities offered by the plasticity of potter's clay were certainly exploited in the creation of these forms, revelations of virtuosity thanks to their surprising structures.''

Pieces of startling originality were born of Picasso's experiments: fantastic, hybrid beasts, in the artist's unmistakable style. These are the dreams of an artist, moulded in ceramics: centaurs, monstrous goats, disconcertingly hieratic birds of prey, bulls with gigantic, threatening horns. And also doves, the

Las Meninas *(the whole). Oil on canvas, Cannes, 1957. (129 × 161 cm). P.M.B.*

Las Meninas *(the whole, excluding Velázquez). Oil on canvas, Cannes, 1957. (130 × 96 cm). P.M.B.*

Las Meninas *(María Agustina Sarmiento). Oil on canvas, Cannes, 1957 (46 × 37.5 cm). P.M.B.*

Las Meninas *(the Infanta Margarita María). Oil on canvas, Cannes, 1957. (46 × 37.5 cm). P.M.B.*

doves so dear to Picasso, in diverse poses, always symbols of peace.

Of the immense quantity of ceramic pieces created by Picasso, we may usefully cite those entitled *Vulture* (1947, Antibes Museum), *Lunar Face on Blue Ground* (1947, Antibes Museum), *Faun's Face* (1948, Antibes Museum), *Picador* (1948, Antibes Museum), *Centaur* (1948, private collection), *Bull* (1948, Antibes Museum), *Dove* (1949, private collection) and *Owl with Outspread Wings* (1957, private collection).

PICASSO THE SCULPTOR

The painter from Málaga always felt an imperious necessity to give the correct value to volumes in his artistic creations, not only in the sculptures, but also in the paintings and ceramics. In the period when he painted the *Portrait of Gertrude Stein* and his *Self-Portrait,* Picasso was primordially concerned to accentuate the illusion of relief on the flat surface of his paintings; in the words of Pierre Daix, ''His desire to paint his subjects' sculptural presence was to lead to a series of authentic painted sculptures, with empty eye sockets, from *Rose Bust* or *Woman with a Chignon* to the splendid, foreshortened *Nude Dressing her Hair,* in the Samuel Marx collection.''

This preoccupation with the perception and represen-

Las Meninas *(Isabel de Velasco). Oil on canvas, Cannes, 1957. (33 × 24 cm). P.M.B.*

Spectators. *Lithograph, 1961. (29.5 × 10.5 cm). P.M.B.*

tation of the dimensions of volumes in his paintings is also palpable in *Les Demoiselles d'Avignon* and, obviously, in all his Cubist oeuvre, in both the Analytical and Synthetic periods. "In fact," stated Roland Penrose, "his Cubism succeeded in uniting both arts — sculpture and painting — in a metaphysical marriage."

Picasso's extensive oeuvre in sculpture — covering a period from approximately 1902 (the date of his first sculpture, now in the Picasso Museum, Barcelona) up to the 1960s, although from 1909 to 1930 he executed practically no sculptures — constitutes an admirable lesson, emphasising the fact that he considered the arts as a unitary phenomenon. Penrose wrote that "Although this duality between the painter and the sculptor is no greater than that opposing the right hand to the left, in his work Picasso created personages to which aspects of himself soon became associated. It is thus reasonable to judge that, by examining these personages, one has the opportunity of to some extent clarifying the two aspects of his personality." There are figures, such as the Harlequin, which Picasso depicted in both painting and sculpture: for example, the canvas entitled *Paulo dressed as a Harlequin,* a portrait of his son painted in 1924, and *Harlequin's Head,* a bronze executed in 1905.

Despite being the author of felicitous phrases as valuable as a treatise on aesthetics, Picasso never needed to have recourse to literature to explain his artistic oeuvre. As an artist, his language was so richly expressive that whenever he wished to clarify anything in the field of creation, he did so by means of images. In many cases his sculptures represented figures and forms that had already been expressed on canvas or paper. The great painter's sculptural works often complement, or explain, concepts that the artist had previously drawn or painted. In his sculptures,

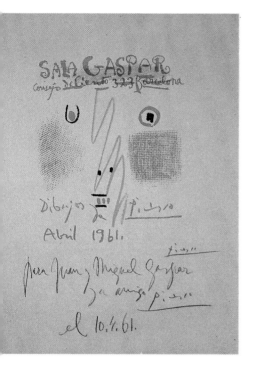

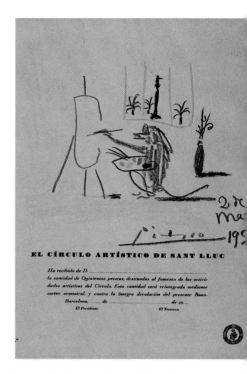

Background of Human Face.
Lithograph in four colours, 1961.
(26 × 18 cm). P.M.B.

Drawings by Picasso. *Lithograph, Sala Gaspar,*
Barcelona, 1961. (71 × 55.5 cm). P.M.B.

Monkey Painter. *Crayon, Mougins,*
1959. (37 × 29 cm). P.M.B.

Picasso showed himself exactly as he was. It would seem that, once he had transferred certain figures onto canvas or paper, the painter felt an imperious necessity to give them corporeity, as if he yearned for their volumes: this was when he turned to sculpture. In the same way as when he painted or worked potter's clay, Picasso devoted himself fully to sculpture when he practised this art form. Penrose wrote that "The sculptor becomes so absolutely absorbed in the contemplation of his work that soon only the sense of touch allows him a sort of contact with his muse. His eyes, which no longer see, are from now on raised to his work and his fingers display a gesture that reminds us of a certain work of the Blue Period, *The Blind Man's Meal,* where blindness finds consolation in the fact that one's hands can touch and caress the objects before one."

Picasso used the most diverse materials in his sculptures (bronze, iron, plaster), sometimes colouring certain works (such as *Glass of Absinthe,* painted bronze, 1914, Museum of Modern Art, New York), covering others with sand, or painting metal plate, as in *Standing Woman* (1961).

A large proportion of Picasso's sculptures were installed at the entrance to the château at Vauvenargues from 1959 onwards; they were later gathered together in the painter's studio at Mougins. Roland Penrose noted that "The sculptures that

Painter at Work. *Oil on canvas, Mougins, 1965.*
(100 × 81 cm). P.M.B.

Bust of Woman with Hat. *Linocut, 1962.*
(63.5 × 52.5 cm). P.M.B.

never found their final positions at Vauvenargues were brought here and again without any attempt at display they were crowded together in the vaults of what had been the entrance hall, joined by others, big and small. Among these were fragile Cubist sculptures, some in poor condition, that had been retrieved after years in storage. A more unexpected intrusion was the arrival of a present from the Antibes Museum of two full-size casts of Michelangelo's slaves. Their bonds seemed all the more intolerable when compared to the revolutionary freedom of the sculpture that surrounded them."

Picasso's best-known sculptures include *Glass of Absinthe* (bronze, 1914, in the Museum of Modern Art, New York), *Man with a Sheep* (1944, installed in a square in Vallauris), *Owl, Goat* (both in bronze, 1950),

Crane (painted bronze, 1951) and *Goat's Skull and Bottle* (bronze, 1951-1952, Museum of Modern Art, New York).

PICASSO AND 20TH-CENTURY ART

The break with the representational convention in painting — the imposition of copying from life that had been in force for centuries — was gradually matured throughout the 19th century, from Goya's "black paintings" to the Impressionists and the Expressionists, in particular. Picasso's achievement was really no more — and no less — than to give the coup de grâce to an aesthetic doctrine that was formally

Bearded Man. *Linocut, 1962. (35 × 27 cm). P.M.B.* ▷

Monument to Picasso in Málaga.

Seated Woman. *Bronze, Barcelona, 1902.*
(15 × 11.5 × 8.5 cm). P.M.B.

out of date, obsolete and impotent in terms of creation.

Painting as a representation of life had been condemned to death since the appearance of photography. The art form could no longer be practised within the same canons as in previous centuries. It was necessary to paint in a different style. This was what Picasso did: rejecting both photographical reproduction and the systematic research that leads to artistic abstraction, following instead a new aesthetic path, that of the "interior monologue" freeing creative expression from archaic restrictions. The artist made this very clear — in words, just as he demonstrated it in his oeuvre when he stated: "The idea of 'searching' has often

made the art of painting fall into abstraction. This has, perhaps, been the greatest error of modern art. The spirit of search has poisoned those who, without understanding all the aspects of modern art, want to paint the invisible, not the pictorial. In many cases the work expresses more than the author wished — he is often astonished by results he had not foreseen. At times these works are the fruit of a kind of spontaneous generation. Sometimes the drawing gives rise to the subject, at others the colour suggests forms that determine the theme." Picasso thus stated an important truth — gratuitously taken as a jest — when he said that he painted what he found, not what he sought, and that in art there are neither specific nor abstract forms, only interpretations.

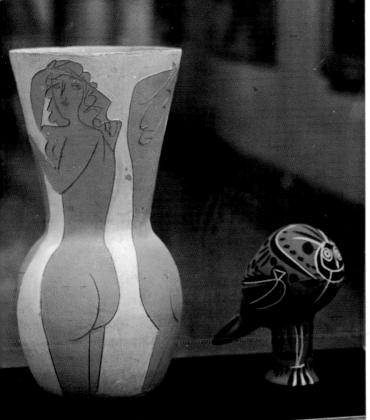

PICASSO'S DENOUNCEMENT OF THE HORRORS OF WAR

Faced with the atrocities committed first in the Spanish Civil War and, immediately afterwards, in the Second World War, Picasso shuddered to the depths of his heart and reacted by firmly condemning violence and arbitrary outrages.

In 1937, at the height of the Spanish Civil War, Picasso sent a message to the Congress of American Republican Artists, in which he clearly expressed his position with regard to the conflict: "I have always believed, and still believe, that artists who live and work in accordance with spiritual values cannot, and must not, remain indifferent to a conflict where the supreme values of humanity and civilisation are at stake." The painter sided with the Republican cause. Rafael Alberti wrote a fine poem on Picasso's attitude in the years of the Spanish Civil War:

La guerra: la española
¿Cuál será la arrancada
del toro que le parte en la cruz una pica?
*   Banderillas de fuego.*
*   Una ola, otra ola desollada.*
*   Guernica.*
*   Dolor al rojo vivo.*
…Y aquí el juego del arte comienza a ser un juego ex-
*   [plosivo.*

Pablo Picasso felt the distinctly Spanish nature in his blood when the tragic events that covered Spain with blood occurred, from 1936 to 1939. Spain was martyrised and the painter, far from feeling unrelated to the tragedy or contemplating it in an egotistical manner, suffered it in his interior and projected his feel-

Man with a Sheep *(bronze sculpture installed in a square in Vallauris). 1944.*

ings in his artistic production. He believed that justice was on the Republican side and accepted to collaborate with the Republican government, on whose commission he painted the famous canvas *Guernica.* Picasso was later also to declare his solidarity with the nations opposing Hitler's Germany, and to condemn the Nazi fascists' agression. Picasso was reported to the Nazis by the painter Vlaminck during the occupation of France by Hitler's troops. He was accused of being a cosmopolitan degenerate; it was even suspected that he had Jewish origins. When he was asked whether he had Jewish blood, he replied that he had not, but added bravely that he would like to have.

It seems that when the painter lived in Nazi-occupied Paris, the German ambassador Abetz went to see him and to enquire about his position. After distastefully observing a photo of *Guernica* in the studio, the Nazi ambassador asked the author of the famous painting: "Did you do this?"

Picasso is said to have replied coldly,

"No... you did."

Paul Eluard, the poet, stated that Pablo Picasso had been one of the few artists who behaved with total dignity during the Germans' occupation of France. Earlier, in 1939, the extraordinary Surrealist poet, with whom Picasso maintained a close friendship, wrote this highly favourable comment in his work *Donner à Voir:* "Of all men who best have experienced their lives and of whom it can never be said that they were present on the earth without immediately realising that they would stay there, Pablo Picasso must be placed amongst the greatest. After conquering the world, he had the courage to rebel against himself." The wars in Korea and Vietnam, with their consequent horrors, also affected Picasso's sensibility and perturbed his spirit, causing the painter to express in

Guernica. *Paris, 1937. (351 × 782 cm). Casón del Buen Retiro, Madrid.*

his art his denouncement and condemnation of the atrocities and injustices committed in the course of the two conflicts.

The great painter's decidedly anti-war stance and his profound love of peace inspired such works as *Guernica, The Charnel House* (exhibited in homage ''to the Spaniards who died for France'' in the Art and Resistance show at the Museum of Modern Art in Paris in 1946) and *Massacre in Korea,* among others, in which his denouncement of the horrors of war is always manifest. As if in compensation, Picasso's dove — an artistic motif that had attracted the young painter as early as his first steps in art in Corunna — has become a universal symbol of peace.

Guernica is undoubtedly the most pathetic of all the pictures painted by Picasso in reaction against war,

violence, and their horrific consequences. It is also the most famous, and is considered to be his masterpiece (in this respect it should be pointed out that the artist created more than one masterpiece). Apart from the specific event inspiring *Guernica* — the destruction by bombing of the Basque town that gave its name to the canvas, perpetrated by the Nazi air force on April 26th 1937 — the painting has become a universal symbol of the violence and barbarity unleashed by warfare. It constitutes a deeply moved, stirring cry for freedom and also, in the words of William Boeck, ''a dreadful inculpation of violence whose ultima ratio is destruction.''

Guernica is an enormous work (351 by 782.5 cm), painted in tempera on canvas. The grey, white and pale green tones contribute to the reflection of a hallucinatory, insuperably dramatic atmosphere. The canvas seems to be devastated, in all senses, by a storm of absolute violence. From one side a bull, surprised or possibly ready to charge, contemplates the radical, boundless destruction prevailing before it while, in the centre, a horse neighs with pain, exposing its teeth, one cannot say whether from rage or distress. On the ground, human figures in pathetic postures, rent with suffering and terror. On the far side from the bull, a masculine face seems to be enjoying the Dantesque spectacle.

The symbolism of this great work by Picasso has been interpreted in many different ways. For the poet Juan Larrea, the painting has a clearly political content, within which the bull represents the Spanish people protecting a woman and a child, the figure of a bird is a representation of the spirit, and the lamp by the window symbolises the Spanish Republic. Larrea, who wrote a magnificent book on *Guernica,* asked Picasso if it was true that the horse in the painting was an allegorical representation of Francoism; the painter replied in the affirmative. On another occasion he asked the same question again and the author of the canvas answered,

"You would have to be blind (or stupid or an art critic, etc.) not to see that."

"Why, then, did you let it be said in an interview that the horse represents the people?"

Picasso replied,

"Why contradict anyone? The Falangist people. Wasn't a part of the people on Franco's side?"

According to Jerome Seckler, the artist said in 1945 that the bull embodied brutality and darkness, while the horse represented the people. In his explanations to the art dealer Kahnweiler in 1947, however, Picasso said that "The bull is a bull and the horse is a horse."

Russell, the author of one of the latest books about Picasso published, says that *Guernica,* like all great works of art, is open to diverse, even contradictory, interpretations. According to Russell, themes of bullfighting — of which the painter was so fond — could explain no few of the enigmas posed by the interpretation of the famous picture's symbolism. As a possible key to its interpretation he also indicates the crucifixion motif, which has in common with the corrida the suffering, mockery and, finally, immolation of an innocent victim.

Picasso himself once said, with his characteristic lucidity, "It would be highly interesting to fix photographically, not the successive stages of a painting, but its successive changes. In this way one might perhaps understand the mental process leading to the embodiment of the artist's dream." Only thus would it be possible to interpret with the necessary rigour such a complex work, rich in suggestions.

Guernica was deposited in the Museum of Modern Art, New York, for many years. After a long process of negotiation with the directors of the said Museum, and with Picasso's heirs (some of whom were against the work's being delivered to Spain), the Spanish Government succeeded in recovering *Guernica* (which had been commissioned from the artist by the Republican Government, when Josep Renau was Director General of Fine Arts): the valuable canvas has been exhibited in the Casón del Buen Retiro, Madrid, since October 1981, although forming part of the Prado Museum's collections.

As well as *Guernica,* other works by Picasso inspired in the condemnation of war include *The Charnel House* (1945, Walter P. Chrysler collection, New York), reflecting the atrocities committed in Nazi concentration camps; *War* (oil on panel, 1952, in Picasso's private collection in 1971), installed alongside *Peace* in an old chapel at Vallauris which the artist acquired and named the "Temple of Peace"; and *Massacre in Korea* (oil on wood, dated 1951), depicting a group of naked women and children preparing to die before the soldiers facing them.

Contents

ACKNOWLEDGMENTS:

The publishers wish to thank the Directors of the Picasso Museum, Barcelona, and its Photography and Documentation Departments, for their invaluable assistance in the preparation of this book.

ESCUDO DE ORO, S.A. COLLECTIONS

EDITORIAL ESCUDO DE ORO, S.A.
14th Edition - I.S.B.N. 84-378-0926-6
Printed by FISA - Escudo de Oro, S.A.
Palaudarias, 26 - 08004 Barcelona
e-mail:editorial@eoro.com
http://www.eoro.com
Dep. Legal B. 1574-2000

Protegemos el bosque; papel procedente de cultivos forestales controlados
Wir schützen den Wald. Papier aus kontrollierten Forsten.
We protect our forests. The paper used comes from controlled forestry plantations
Nous sauvegardons la forêt: papier provenant de cultures forestières contrôlées

The printing of this book was completed
in the workshops of
FISA - ESCUDO DE ORO, S.A.
Palaudarias, 26 - Barcelona (Spain)